Friendliness

BY CYNTHIA AMOROSO

Published by The Child's World®
1980 Lookout Drive • Mankato, MN 56003-1705
800-599-READ • www.childsworld.com

Acknowledgments
The Child's World®: Mary Berendes, Publishing Director
The Design Lab: Design
Pamela J. Mitsakos: Photo Research
Christine Florie: Editing

Photographs ©: Brand X Pictures: 5; David M. Budd Photography: 7, 11, 13, 17, 21; iStockphoto.com/gbh007: 9; Hart Creations: cover, 1; iStockphoto.com/NadyaPhoto: 19; iStockphoto.com/SergiyN: 15.

ISBN 9781623235185
LCCN 2013931442

Printed in the United States of America
Mankato, MN
July, 2013
PA02172

ABOUT THE AUTHOR

Cynthia Amoroso is Director of Curriculum and Instruction for a school district in Minnesota. She enjoys reading, writing, gardening, traveling, and spending time with friends and family.

Table of Contents

What Is Friendliness?

Friendliness means treating other people nicely. It means being kind and warm to people. Friendliness means smiling or saying hello. Friendliness makes you happy! It makes other people happy, too.

Friendliness makes you feel good!

Friendliness at School

Imagine that your class has a new student. Being the new kid can be scary. You can tell that the new student feels shy. You show friendliness by smiling at her. You talk to her after class. You **introduce** her to your friends.

Friendliness can make a new student feel welcome.

Friendliness Can Lead to New Friends

You and your friends love to play on the swings. One day, a boy walks over. He stands by the swing set. He waits quietly for his turn. You show friendliness by smiling and saying hello. You give him your swing when you are done. You introduce him to your friends. Now you have a new friend!

Asking someone to play is a way of being friendly.

Friendliness Can Cheer You Up

It is Monday morning. You feel tired and crabby. You walk into the kitchen. Your parents are sitting at the table. You do not really feel like talking. You smile and say good morning anyway. You visit with your parents. Slowly, you start to cheer up. Friendliness has made your day brighter!

You can be friendly even when you do not feel like it.

Friendliness Can Cheer Others Up

You get to school early. You can tell that your teacher is grumpy. You show friendliness by smiling at her. You visit with her for a little while. You ask her if she had a good weekend. Your teacher starts to smile. Your friendliness has cheered her up.

Being friendly to your teacher will start her day off right.

Little Kids Need Friendliness, Too

You had a long day at school. You are tired when you get home. Your little brother runs to greet you. He smiles and brings you his **favorite** book. You do not really feel like reading with him. You show friendliness by reading with your brother anyway.

Being friendly to your family can make you feel good.

Friendliness Can Be Small Things

Your sister does not feel very good. She is just getting over a cold. You ask her if she would like to do something. She does not feel like playing yet. She still feels tired. She does not feel like going outside. You show friendliness just by being with her.

Being friendly shows your sister that you are also her friend.

Friendliness Helps Those Who Are Lonely

Do you have an **elderly** neighbor who lives alone? Maybe you see him raking his leaves. Maybe you see him working in his garden. You can tell he is a little lonely. You show friendliness by waving to him. You smile at him and say hello.

Helping others is a great way to show friendliness.

Friendliness Is for Everyone!

Friendliness is not just for friends. It helps your family, teachers, and neighbors, too. Friendliness makes other people feel good. It also makes you feel good. Friendliness makes the world a nicer place!

Being friendly to our neighbors makes everyone happy.

Glossary

elderly–When someone is elderly, they are older.

favorite–When you like something best, it is your favorite.

introduce–To introduce people is to help them meet each other.

Learn More

Books

Adams, Christine A. *Learning to Be a Good Friend: A Guidebook for Kids*. St. Meinrad, IN: Abbey Press, 2004.

Brown, Laurie Krasny. *How to Be a Friend: A Guide to Making Friends and Keeping Them*. Boston: Little, Brown, 1998.

Meiners, Cheri J. *Be Polite and Kind*. Minneapolis, MN: Free Spirit, 2004.

Web Sites

Visit our Web site for links about friendliness: childsworld.com/links

Note to Parents, Teachers, and Librarians: We routinely verify our Web links to make sure they are safe and active sites. So encourage your readers to check them out!

Index